ENDLESS
INTERNET PROFITS

A STEP-BY-STEP BLUEPRINT TO BUILDING AN INTERNET BUSINESS THAT WILL GENERATE EVERLASTING, PASSIVE PROFITS

Disclaimer

CHAPTER 1: The Endless Internet Profits – What You'll Learn

There are many different types of business models you can start today. Some are seasonal, that is, most sales occur during a particular time of year. Others have sales spread out throughout the year but require frequent and active management.

> *While there's no wrong type of business – as long as you're turning a profit – an evergreen, passive model of business is one of the best there is.*

Imagine being away on holiday. You're on a sailboat, or you're backpacking somewhere on the other side of the world. When you get an Internet connection, you check your PayPal account or your bank account, and you hear that cha-ching sound.

It's a sight to behold - you've earned hundreds or thousands of dollars in the 8 hours you've been away from your computer. Sounds like a dream, right?

You didn't have to trade your time for money, and you get to do what you love. And you still earned passive income that's more than what most people make in a month!

Wouldn't you like to have this kind of business?

I'm sure you would. Or else you won't be reading this guide.

Now, this step-by-step blueprint is going to cover all the details about building an Internet business that will generate everlasting, passive profits for you.

At this point, I'd like to make it clear to you that success is not going to happen overnight. This is certainly not a get rich quick scheme.

Building a profitable Internet business takes a lot of time. There are just far too many factors to consider before you can succeed.

If you've been listening to gurus who tell you that you can get rich in 24 hours or 3 days, then you've got another think coming. Those gurus are out to get your money, nothing more. Income reports can easily be faked so don't believe everything you see.

In this blueprint, I'm not going to be putting up income screenshots – I'll leave that to the fake gurus. Instead, I'll show you everything there is to know about building an evergreen Internet business. I'll teach you the methods and principles that are working now and into the future.

Some concepts may be new to you, but I'll do my best to walk you through each topic, so the learning curve isn't as steep and as difficult.

Here's a quick summary of what you can expect to learn in this series:

1. You'll know about the best evergreen niches you can explore for your business. I'll give you plenty of options, but ultimately, the decision to choose the right niche will fall on you.

2. You'll learn why it's important to have a goal in mind and why you need to sit down, brainstorm, and create a real business plan and strategy. This will be your evergreen business foundation. Without a solid foundation, there's a chance your business won't last a year.

3. You'll understand the importance of branding and why businesses – both big and small – pay huge sums of money to advertise their brand. Don't worry though, you don't need to go broke to do this. I'll teach you a few strategies you can use without breaking the bank!

4. You'll know why establishing an online social presence, and online identity is important for your business. If you shy away from social media, then it's time to take a deep breath and dive into it head first because there's really no getting around this one.

Unless you have the money to hire a social media manager, then you must do this on your own, at least in the beginning.

5. You'll find out how to create valuable content that sticks and resonates with your audience. Creating content that actually matters is important – you have to do a lot of research, so you know you're actually hitting and addressing your audience's pain points.

6. You'll learn why recycling or repurposing content is a must if you want to maximize your efforts and extend your reach. And no, I'm not talking about copying and pasting your content in its entirety. I'm referring to converting your content into other formats so you can upload it to other platforms.

This helps expand your reach so people on those platforms will also find your content. Sound vague? Don't worry, I'll give you the details, I promise.

7. You'll know how to generate traffic from many different sources – from forums, question and answer sites, to various social media platforms. You're going to seek out your target audience on these platforms so you can get eyes to your valuable content.

You don't even have to pay for traffic, but if you've got the budget for it, I'll cover both free and paid traffic sources just to give you options.

8. You'll find out why building a mailing list goes hand in hand with building your business. When I say mailing list, I mean an e-mailing list. After all, we are living in the digital age, and people would rather give out their email address than their physical address!

You'll know several techniques to get people to give you their email address, and before you know it, you'll have hundreds or thousands of subscribers on your list!

9. You'll know the different ways you can create and sell your very own evergreen course. There are many different kinds of products you can make and I'll go through all the popular ones that work with a wide variety of people.

Once you know how to make your own product, then I'll show you where you can sell it to get those dollars coming into your account so you can start living your dream life!

Yes, there's a lot of ground to cover in this blueprint. You just need to have the patience to go through everything. Don't be afraid to take notes.

Print out this guide if you so wish and make it your very own blueprint to success. And don't stop at reading and taking notes. You've got to take action.

Go out and do all the steps I'm going to be sharing with you. You may fail in your first few attempts at building an evergreen business, but with every failure, you'll be learning.

I didn't say this is going to be easy, but I promise you, at the end of this series of chapters, you'll know everything there is to know about how to build an online business that you and your family can live off of for many, many years to come.

CHAPTER 2: How To Find An Evergreen Niche You'll Stick With

Building a business is hard. Finding an evergreen niche you want to build your business on is even harder. Sure, you can just go and pick a random niche anytime you like, but would you be able to devote or spend the time necessary to grow your business?

If you answered no, then you might have chosen the wrong niche. If you answered yes, then you might have a gem on your hands. After all, finding success in an evergreen niche can mean a passive income stream for you for many years to come.

How To Find The Right Evergreen Niche

There are literally thousands upon thousands of niches and sub-niches you can choose for your business. Not everything's going to be profitable though. And certainly, not all niches are evergreen. Some may be seasonal, while some fad niches may last only a few weeks or a few months – these aren't the niches you're looking for.

Evergreen niches are those that don't depend on the time of year, or even the year itself. Popular evergreen products continue to sell years, or even decades, after it was first sold. If you find the right evergreen niche, and target the right audience with the right product, you could be making a lot of money.

When looking for the perfect evergreen niche for your business, you basically have two options: Profit or Passion. Different people will give you different answers, so you'd have to really look inside yourself to find the right answer. There's no right or wrong answer, mind you, but to help you weigh your options, here are the pros and cons of each.

Option 1. Choose A Niche You're Passionate About

Most beginners actually choose this option. Why? Because they are already passionate about a particular topic, and they are confident they can write long-form articles or content around the subject.

If you have a favorite hobby or something that really perks you up every time you come across that subject, then you might want to look deeper and see if you can create a business off of that. You know what they say, right? Do what you love, and you'll never work another day in your life.

You can write a 5,000-word article on the subject every week and publish it on your site, that's how passionate you are about the topic. Or if you're into publishing info products, then having the commitment and the passion to producing quality content regularly will contribute greatly to your success.

Having the passion for your subject is obviously important. Otherwise, your interest is going to fizzle out after a few weeks when you realize just how hard it is to build a business from scratch!

But your passion will see you through, and carry you through the rough days. Because yes, there will be rough days. It's just a fact of life that not even passion niches can escape from.

Now, one of the downsides to choosing a niche based on passion is that after a while – no matter how much you love the subject – you may eventually start to resent the work. During the course of your research, or after you've written a hundred thousand words on the topic, you'll feel burnt out.

If you have the money, however, the option to outsource the grunt work is always there. But generally speaking, beginners who choose to go this route don't usually have the budget.

Another downside to option 1, depending on the hobby or interest you're building an evergreen product for, is that there may not be a whole lot of people interested in the subject.

While you could potentially make sales year-round, the volume may not be up to par as compared to choosing a niche for profit. If you'd like to cut to the chase and build a business on a profitable niche, then read the next section for ideas.

Option 2. Choosing A Niche For Profit

The second option will take a lot more work than the first. You'd have to do plenty of research to identify a potentially profitable niche. You'd have to study trends, do plenty of keyword research, and generally have your ear to the ground to find out what's popular and making sales.

You have to pay attention to the news and look for something that will grab your attention and make you go, "I can sell that!"

When choosing a niche for profit, you might think it's going to be hard creating content for something you may not know anything about. You can, of course, do plenty of research – you can do desktop research by going on

Google, or if you want first-hand information, you can even interview industry experts!

Doing this may take you plenty of time. If you want to avoid the long wait, you may want to consider hiring an expert in the subject area. Or hire a freelancer who can do the research and the write-up for you. Of course, choosing the right freelancer will also take time.

They're also not going to come cheap, so you'd need to consider this as well. But if money's not an issue, then going for option 2 is a very smart business decision.

Choosing a niche for profit takes a lot of uncertainty out of the equation. Unlike choosing a passion niche which may or may not translate to a nice volume of sales, choosing a profitable niche is designed to help you make the most amount of profit.

With luck, you may even find a profitable niche that you're interested in – this is the best of both worlds! For best results, a *profitable* evergreen niche you're *passionate* about is something you should strive to look for.

Remember, at the end of the day, you're creating a business to make money. It makes sense to choose a niche you know is going to be more profitable than a niche you may love but is not going to be as profitable.

The Top Evergreen Niches You Should Consider For Your Business

In this section, I will show you some of the most popular niches that always sells and are always popular. These are massive niches where you can find plenty of sub-niches. If you drill down far enough, you're going to find a sub-niche not many people are talking about and offering solutions to.

This is what you came here to find. I'm going to try my best and point you in the right direction so you can start thinking about the niche you'd eventually like to build your business on!

Health Niche

This is one of the biggest niches where successful entrepreneurs make millions and even billions of dollars annually. And I'm not even talking about those huge pharmaceutical companies – I'm talking about the small and medium-sized entrepreneurs and startups.

If you'd like a share of this money-making pie, then dive into this niche!

Here are some of the sub-niches you can focus on:

Fitness and weight loss/gain – there will always be people interested in getting fit and losing or gaining weight. I am pretty sure that everyone, at one point in our lives, has researched about ways to lose weight or build muscles – that includes you and me!

Diet and nutrition – another extremely popular sub-niche. Some diets have stood the test of time. Others not so much. With so many people wanting to know the easiest way to lose weight, different diet programs will continue to crop up for years to come!

Cures for diseases – there are so many ailments that befall the human body. If you know of a solution to a specific condition that not too many people are discussing, then you may want to develop a product based on that!

Exercise – there are plenty of exercise routines and exercise equipment that are available to the public right now. If you like this niche, you can create exercise videos and grow your business around it.

You can upload your videos to YouTube and monetize it there, or you can create a membership program on your website and give members exclusive access to your videos.

Feel free to explore and go even deeper in the health sub-niches. Think outside the box. The more specific the health problems you can address, the less competition you'll have, and the easier your road to success will be.

Wealth Niche

Everyone wants to learn how to make money. Without money, we can't live the life we want to live. We can't reach for our dreams. We'll be forever tied to low paying jobs and caught in the never-ending rat race. Wealth gives us the freedom to do the things we love with the people we want to share the moment with.

Just like the health niche, there are plenty of sub-niches you can tackle in the wealth niche. Here's a few of them:

How to make money online – in this niche, you'll find plenty of competition. There are countless ways to make money online – you can build a blog, create info products, work as a freelancer, teach English as a second language to overseas students, sell merchandise online, dropship, and so much more. If you know of a proven way to make money online, don't be afraid to share your knowledge with the world.

How to make money offline – not everyone's into making money online. Some people are still into traditional ways of making money offline. If you've got ideas on how you can help people earn some extra dough without using the Internet, share it! It just may be your next passive income stream.

Personal Finance – being financially fit is an important topic that people from all walks of life can benefit from. We all need money. And knowing how to save and spend money wisely is a topic that will remain relevant for as long as we use money in our daily lives.

Investments – there's a lot of risks involved with any kind of investment, but there will always be people interested in knowing the different techniques in trading and investing in various commodities. If you've got specialized knowledge or experience in these areas, you may want to consider building your evergreen product in this niche!

Personal Development Niche

Another very popular evergreen niche is the personal development niche. This is a vast niche simply because there are so many areas we want to improve ourselves on.

We are constantly looking for ways to improve our attitude, our appearance, our organizational skills, our personal and professional relationships, self-discipline, and so much more.

The thing with personal development is that it's a lifelong process. You want to build yourself and your skills for the long haul – that's why it's called development. It's a work in progress, so to speak. You're making a conscious effort to develop yourself so you can reach your long-term goals.

If you'd like to build your business in this niche, here are some good sub-niches you may want to consider:

Leadership skills – people respect and look up to leaders whether it be in a professional setting, a religious setting, political, etc. Leaders often make good decisions and are in the position to solve problems, both big and small. If you think you can teach other people how to become a great leader, then this might be the perfect niche for you.

Communication skills - having excellent communication skills can open many doors for you. This includes knowing how to listen and how to speak in public. You can teach people how to get ahead of their competition by simply working on their communication skills.

Confidence – everyone needs confidence. Shy and meek people may not get very far in life because they're too shy to jump on an opportunity. When you're confident, it's easier for you to succeed because you believe in yourself – you can easily overcome your fears and your doubts.

When you exude confidence, you appear more trustworthy, and people feel they can trust whatever it is you're saying.

Job interview skills – in order to land your dream job, you need to have excellent job interview skills to stand out from the competition. You need to have the confidence and the communication skills to snag that job.

If you think you have what it takes to teach people how to ace job interviews, then this might be the right niche for you.

Finding the right evergreen niche to build your business on will take time.

You have to invest in the right tools, and you need to have the patience to uncover those special niches which will generate everlasting profits for you.

CHAPTER 3: How To Build A Foundation You Can Build On Forever

Businesses can be built overnight – some even materialize in just a few hours! But more often than not, businesses like these don't last for a long time. They'd probably be profitable for a few months, but once problems start happening as they often do during the early stages of a business, then they'd fold up, surrender, and disappear.

I'm sure you don't want that to happen to your business. If you want your business to stand the test of time, then you need to think it through very carefully.

> *You need to build a solid foundation before you even start offering your evergreen product or services to your target audience.*

Let's use a skyscraper analogy. If you want to build a skyscraper, or any building for that matter, you need to build a solid foundation first. You'd need to dig deep into the earth until you find a more stable subsoil or bedrock, put steel and other hard materials on it, and then pour concrete over everything.

Of course, a lot more work goes into building a skyscraper's foundation, but that's about the gist of it. When the foundation's dried up, only then can you start working on your skyscraper – the building above ground.

No one really sees all the hard work that goes into building a foundation, but its importance cannot be downplayed. Without a solid foundation, your skyscraper is going to fall down either on its own or the next time an earthquake strikes your city.

Likewise, if you want your evergreen business to last, then you're going to have to put in a lot of work and map out your road to success. No matter how small your business is, you still need a roadmap, so you don't veer off into unwanted directions, particularly bankruptcy.

You need to answer a lot of if-then scenarios and put it all down on paper – "*if this happens, then this is what I'm going to do*." Put safeguards in place. If you have a business partner, you need to brainstorm and plan out every detail of your business.

But what if you've already started your business? Is it too late to build a foundation?

Well, the answer depends on where you are in your business. If you haven't reached the point of no return – and only you know where that point is – you can still make adjustments and map out a foundation to turn your business around and give it new life.

The Checklist To Building A Solid Foundation For Your Business

If you want to build a solid foundation for your evergreen business, you should be able to tick off most items on the list. Let's begin!

Make It A Goal To Help As Many People As Possible

Identifying your business goals right off the bat is important. I know making a profit is the ultimate goal but don't stop at money. I'm not saying money isn't important – it is. But it's not the end goal.

Your ultimate goal should be to help other people. As the great salesman Zig Ziglar famously said, "*You will get all you want in life if you help enough other people get what they want.*"

If you're only doing your business for money, then people are going to know about it soon enough. They're going to stop buying from you, and they're going to tell their friends to stay away from you. Greed is not going to get you very far in life.

Look at what happens to so-called gurus – they'd be profitable for a few months but once word gets out that they're not really in the business of helping, then these gurus disappear.

> *But if you follow Mr. Ziglar's advice, and do your best to help people, then you'll have more money than you know what to do with!*

For example, if you want to create evergreen products, make sure that those products are actually helping people solve their problems. Don't sell for the sake of selling. If you focus on helping people, then you'll have loyal customers coming to buy your products over and over again.

They'll refer you to their family and friends, and if you continue to provide the same level of service, then they'll be your loyal customers, too. And before you know it, you'll have plenty of money in the bank than you know what to do with!

Having other business goals is perfectly fine. Just remember to always put your customers first. After all, they're the reason you're in business. All the other points in this checklist should also tie in with your overall goal of helping people.

Having concrete plans and solid systems in place mean nothing if you can't deliver what your customers need help with. They are the lifeblood of your business so take good care of them. When you do this, you will no longer need to think of money constantly as people will give it to you willingly!

Have A Business Plan In Place

Some first-time entrepreneurs may say having a business plan for a small business is overkill. But if you want your business to grow and scale eventually, then it's best to have a business plan in place. It's not too late to write one so if you haven't got a plan yet, then take the time to write it up and see where your business is going to be in the future.

One of the advantages of creating a business plan, before you even start working on your business, is that you can determine right away if your idea is feasible or not. You could, of course, just wing it and go right out and implement your business idea.

> But if you value your time and money, then this may not be the best route for you to follow.

A business plan has a section on competitive analysis or market analysis. At this stage, you should be able to assess if your idea is a good one or not. Just imagine how much resources you would have wasted if you decided to try out your idea in the real world only for it to fail miserably!

Investing in the time to work on your business plan will help ensure a smoother startup period, and you'll know what problems to expect. Yes, you'll still run into some unforeseen problems here and there, but if you did your business plan correctly, then you should already have mapped out solutions to most problems.

For instance, you would have an idea of how much money you need to invest so you can start or scale your business. If you fly by the seat of your pants, you may not get very far. Unforeseen expenses could come into play even before you break even and you may be forced to quit your fledgling business.

Your business plan is like your crystal ball – if you believe in that stuff – as it allows you to practically get a glimpse of your future. If the future looks bleak for your idea, then scrap that and move on to the next one.

However, if the future looks bright then, by all means, go ahead and build your business right away. Your business plan has already foretold good tidings, the next thing for you to do is further solidify your foundation by moving on to the actual business building part!

Separate Your Personal Life From Your Business

Most entrepreneurs start by being a one-person team. You do everything in your business – you create your product, you market it, you do customer service and after-sales support, and so much more. You're going to be a jack of all trades literally.

In the beginning, it's going to be hard to separate your personal life from your business life. You might not have boundaries for your business and personal expenses, and that's fine. But if you're serious about growing your business, then you need to find a way to separate your two lives.

If you work out of your bedroom, or any other room in your house, as plenty of new entrepreneurs do, then you most certainly need to have rules in place.

You'll need to have a designated workspace where you focus a hundred percent on doing the tasks for the day. Make your family or roommate understand work time is for working, not playing. Put a "do not disturb" sign outside your door if you have to. Lock the door or put on a good pair of headphones, so you don't get bothered by the outside world.

To successfully separate your personal and business lives, you'd need to have self-discipline. I mean, how easy is it to walk over to the couch and watch Netflix the whole day instead of answering emails from your customers?

You're probably thinking you can bring your laptop over to the couch and multi-task. But do you think you're really going to be productive that way? I don't think so.

If you can't keep your two lives separate, then you're not going to have a very solid foundation for your evergreen business. Even if you do work at home, or in an office, or even at the beach, you need to draw the line between fun and work so your business will succeed in the long run.

Have Systems In Place

Having a good business plan in place means you've already got some basic systems in place. But when it comes to streamlining your business and making the most of your resources, you need to have highly effective and efficient systems in place.

When you're just starting, your systems may not be as defined. Sure, you can plan ahead, but the nitty gritty is not going to materialize until you finally start working on your business. You may need to adjust your plans as you go along because working off of theory and practice are two different things.

When you're working off of theory alone, you're not in touch with the practical side of things. Some systems may look good on paper, but when it actually comes to following those systems, they're not going to be as efficient and may cost you a lot of time and money.

So, you need to adjust accordingly and tweak your system to be as efficient as possible. Don't set your systems in stone, you need to be flexible and adapt as needed.

Building working systems are essential to solidifying your business foundation. For example, identifying your marketing and product delivery systems is essential to your success.

You may need to undergo some trial and error first to find the best system that works for you, but once that's out of the way, you now have a winning system in place. You can then use that system over and over again as you move forward with your business.

Don't forget to document your systems. You may think you're working all alone, so you don't need to document everything. But what about when you finally gain some traction, and you need to hire new people to help you out?

Without documentation, you'd need to retrace your steps, and because you're under time pressure, you might miss out on a few key steps. However, if you're proactive with documenting your processes and your systems, then you can start training your new team as soon as you hire them!

Are You Ready To Start Building Your Foundation?

Building a solid foundation for your business will take time. If you're in a hurry and you decide to jump the gun without having a solid plan in place, then you may end up regretting your decision. If you want your business to last for years and years, then investing in a solid foundation is the best thing for you to do.

Now the common misconception for business foundations is that it's irrevocable and final. Fortunately, it's not. You can adjust and recalibrate your plans if you need to. A solid foundation will allow you to do just that.

Many companies who failed to adjust and adapt to changing times and technologies have disappeared. If you're in the business of helping people – and not just making plenty of money – then you've got the most solid foundation right there.

CHAPTER 4: How To Create A Personal Or Business Brand That People Will Trust

If you've ever bought anything from anyone online, then you know it's pretty normal to hop on to Google and do a quick search of the person or company you're doing business with. It's normal to be curious about a person, especially if money is going to change hands.

You'd probably click through all the web links that Google gives you, read all you can about the person or company so you can determine if it's a good idea to do business with them. In the old days, you'd probably ask for a referral, call that person and ask them for their opinion or personal experiences with that particular person or business.

During the course of your research, you'll form an opinion about the person. Are they trustworthy? Are they credible? What do other people say about them? Have they ever scammed anyone?

These questions are asked by people unfamiliar with you and your business. It's nothing personal, of course, it's just a normal way of doing business nowadays. In this chapter,

I will explain the importance of branding – why you need to do it and how to build a brand that people will trust.

What Exactly Is Branding?

Some people may say your company name or your logo is your branding. This may be true for some, but in essence, it goes beyond that. Branding is the overall picture or reputation that people think of when they see your brand.

For instance, if you're in the food business, a certain group of people may associate your brand with their childhood. For another group, they may associate your brand with their kids. There's no single definition of what makes your brand *your brand.*

Branding is highly subjective and will vary from person to person. Some may love your brand, others may not, and so on. While you can't control what other people think of you or your brand, you can certainly push them in the right direction to put your brand in a more positive light.

You can spend a lot of money on a branding campaign. You can buy plenty of ad space portraying your food business as the best source of healthy, nutritious food in your city.

If your campaign goes as planned, then people will remember your brand as a healthy and nutritious brand. But if your campaign goes south, for instance, a customer found something nasty on her food (like an insect), then people may start associating your brand with that nasty insect!

Why Is Branding So Important For Your Business?

Building a brand is non-negotiable. In this day and age where your competitors are not necessarily in the same location as you, you need to stand out from the crowd. Thanks to the Internet, today's marketplace is a global one.

You have literally the whole world to sell your product to. And if you're selling an evergreen product, building a brand right from the get-go is essential if you want your business to generate profits for you for many years.

If you don't take branding seriously, then people are going to choose your competitors over you. The more transparent you are about your business, the more people will trust you. But if you hide behind a façade or even stock photography, then people are going to see right through you.

Of course, you don't have to share everything about your life – you do still have a right to privacy, after all. But the point is that, if you're offering a product or service, let your customers see that you are real.

They don't have to know the minute details of your life, they just need to know they can trust you. Let them have a peek at your personal life if you want, but that's totally up to you.

> *Your reputation will define you and your brand. If you've got a reputation for being professional because you take good care of your customers, then that helps your brand.*

People will start associating your business with a being a consummate professional, and you'll have referrals and repeat customers coming in.

However, if you made quite a number of people unhappy, they're most probably going to leave bad reviews all over the web so when people search for you, they'll see your brand or business is not so reliable, and they'll be better off buying somewhere else.

You don't want this to happen to you. If your brand has been ruined, you can either hire a professional to help clean up your image or start from scratch, if you can. However, do know that nothing ever gets deleted on the Internet so even if you create a new identity or a new brand, someone may still be able to unearth your flaws and past mistakes.

If you want to be in business for a long time, then make sure you build your brand the right way. You need to spend considerable time building your brand but, in the end, the effort will be worth it. Your reputation will precede you, and people will not hesitate to do business with you.

The Top Ways To Create A Personal Or Business Brand People Will Trust

There are plenty of ways to build your brand. But before you can do this, first, you need to find out what the Internet already knows about you

Do a Google search for your name or business. If you're marketing using your own name, type your name both with and without quotes on a private or incognito browser window, so your search results aren't skewed. If you're marketing using your business name, do the same method.

Check out what the search engine gives you. Are you happy with the result? Does it show you in a positive light? Or do you have an angry client or customer up on the first page of Google?

If you don't have any negative comments come up, then that's a great sign! You can continue to build your brand on such a positive result. On the other hand, if you've got some negative comments, do your best to answer professionally to put yourself in a more positive light.

After all, your competitors may have hired people to do a smear job on you to ruin your reputation and scare your customers away from you. Not many people do that, fortunately, but it does happen. So you better make sure all your feedback – positive and negative – are all genuine.

Create an unforgettable experience for each customer you serve

When you deliver personalized service to your customers, people will appreciate you. Make each interaction an experience for your customers. Too many businesses are only out to get their customers' money, they don't really care about them at all. It's important to make yourself stand out and be different.

Another way to create an unforgettable experience for your customers is by engaging with them directly. By treating them as people, you're erasing barriers. You're positioning yourself as someone they can communicate with directly.

This is why even big Fortune 500 companies have people manning their social media channels so when customers bring something to their attention, they're able to respond to it quickly and publicly.

Putting on a face to your company brings you closer to your customers – and they'll pay you back with loyalty.

When you make an impact on your customers' minds, they'll remember you and your actions during those times you engaged with them. They may not remember what they bought from you, but they'll remember your actions and the feelings that your actions evoked.

Build a relationship with your customers

Humans crave relationships, that's a fact. So, when you build a relationship with your customers, you're literally telling them they can count on you. Don't take their trust lightly because the moment you do that, you'll lose that trust.

Once that's lost, it's going to be hard to win it back. More often than not, they'll transfer their trust to your competitors and maybe even convince a number of your customers to go over to the other side, too.

When you build a relationship with your customers, you need to put a lot of effort into making it work. Depending on the nature of your business, you can maybe mail them gifts during special times of the year, offer them a discount code or a free month of your service.

In short, make them feel special. That's how relationships work – you make the other person feel special.

Another aspect of building a relationship with your customers is that you can also build a community or a group for them. Inviting them to join your community may make them feel special. They'll meet new friends, and they'll get to interact even more with your business.

Be personable and authentic

Connecting with your customers is very important. However, hiding behind a fake name or profile is going to be detrimental to your success. You can connect all you want with your customers on social media or on your website, but once word gets out that you're a flake, then you'll lose face.

 You'll lose your credibility, and your reputation may vanish overnight. You'll lose all the customers you've worked so hard to build a relationship with.

Being authentic is one important aspect of building your brand's foundation. If you build a brand on a fake persona, it's going to be hard to grow your business.

Yes, you may find some success, but your growth will be limited. There's always going to be that boundary you can't cross. Otherwise, people will know you're not real, and then you'll lose your brand.

Stay consistent and always follow through

Be visible in places where your customers hang out. If you've got plenty of customers on Facebook, Twitter, Instagram, Snapchat, or any other social media channel your audience frequents, then don't be afraid to reach out to them.

Show them you're active on their favorite platforms and engage with them. Answer their questions. Be their friend. Give them plenty of value for free without asking for anything in return. In their mind, you're an authority figure or a thought leader. They'll trust what you say.

If you're honest and consistent, people will notice. If you tell them you're going to do something, then do that. Document it if you can so they know you've done what you promised. You've got proof to show them.

This is why following through is very important as well. If you don't follow through, you're making empty promises, and soon, people will lose their trust in you. Your word won't mean anything, and you'll lose your audience.

The Best Way To Control Your Brand's Reputation

Controlling what other people see about your brand is not always easy, especially if you've been around for a few years and you've never paid attention to what people are saying about you on the Internet.

You can use social media to interact with your customers and your clients. But at the end of the day, you don't own that platform. You can have all your testimonials on social media, but what if that platform disappears?

Simply put, the best platform to control your brand's reputation is by building your own website. And by your own website, I don't mean getting a free website from a blogging platform. You need your own website with your own domain name which should preferably be your brand name.

It will help if you've got a memorable or brandable domain name too, so it's easier for people to search for you on Google. Getting a domain name and web hosting is very cheap nowadays, and it's one of the best investments you can make for your business.

With your own website, you can control the information you want to share with the world. If you've got positive testimonials from social media, you can post screenshots on your website. If you've got a portfolio on other platforms, bring them over to your website.

Create a forum on your website for your loyal followers or place a link to other channels where they can engage with you. It allows them to see your diversified presence on the Internet and if they're on those other platforms as well, then they'd also follow you there.

It also makes it easier for potential customers to find you when you are referred to them by their friends.

Creating a personal or business brand that people will trust will take a lot of work and a lot of time. The tips I've shared in this chapter will not only point you in the right direction, but will also help you build your brand much faster.

CHAPTER 5: How To Establish An Online Social Presence And Identity

Establishing an online social presence and identity is important nowadays. Gone are the days when your business can go about its merry ways in the offline world. Even if you don't cater to the online crowd – people will still search for your brand or business on Google.

If they don't find you online, they'll look for your competitor who's probably already got an online presence. It doesn't matter if you're 10x or 100x better than your competitors. If people don't find you online, then you might as well not exist.

Having your very own website is important. But more and more people are turning to social media to seek out their favorite brands. If people want to complain about something, they don't go to the company's Contact Us page to write a lengthy complaint email.

Instead, they go to social media and rant their displeasure or disappointment, and basically tell the whole world just how bad a service provider you are. You can see just how much you'd lose if you're not on social media – you can't see or answer those complaints.

People will bury you online without you even knowing it. But you'll likely notice those dwindling revenues on your books, and you won't know why.

Now, if you have social media, and you're actively monitoring it, then you'd be able to answer their concerns, put their minds at ease, offer a return or whatever, and essentially show the world that you provide great customer service.

You can use negative feedback to your advantage by being courteous and showing your professionalism.

What Exactly Is Social Media Presence And Why Is It Important?

Having accounts on various social media platforms doesn't mean you've got a social media presence. To make your social media presence matter, you need to be active by posting valuable content regularly and engaging with your audience.

When I say valuable content, I mean content that's relevant to your brand.

This includes thoughtful posts, comments, updates, and even useful links from competing brands.

You have to show your followers that you are there, that you are in fact present. When they send you a message, reply to them promptly, especially if they post it on your timeline or somewhere other people can see the question, too.

Whether you like it or not, you'll be judged by the timeliness and relevance of your response. Having a solid social media presence allows you to establish yourself as an influencer. If you've got a good reputation, people are more apt to follow what you say. When you recommend something, people trust your recommendation.

Because of this, you'd need to be careful with your recommendations. You have to vet products you recommend, don't just think of the money or the commissions you'll make.

When you see social media "influencers" peddling everything from all walks of life, you'd know they're in it for the money. I'm positive you wouldn't want to follow such an account lest you want to get random sales pitches for anything and everything under the sun.

Try to recommend only products that are actually related to your brand and your products. Choose products that resonate with you personally, your brand, and your audience. If you're in the pets niche, you wouldn't want to recommend products that are totally unrelated to your pets. That would only cause people to unfollow you.

As an influencer, it's your name and your brand on the line. One wrong move could cost you your social media presence and can literally ruin your brand overnight.

However, if you do the influencer thing correctly, it could mean another stream of income for your business, especially if you typically get good conversion rates from your followers.

Providing good value is always essential to any business. If people know you're not going to be selling them random items and are instead recommending useful products, you're going to have them by the palm of your hand, and they'll buy whatever you recommend!

How To Establish Your Social Media Presence And Identity

Creating social media accounts is easy. But establishing your identity and your presence won't happen overnight. It's going to be a full-time job trying to establish a solid presence on social media.

You can probably manage one platform on your own. But if you want wider reach and being active on two, three, or even more social platforms, then using scheduling tools or hiring a social media manager may be your best course of action.

Here are a few tips to get you off to a good start with your social media presence:

Have a goal for your social media presence

There are lots of reasons why brands should have a social media presence. For instance, you can use it to educate and inform potential customers about your brand. You can use it as an avenue for customer service or technical support.

You can even use it to generate leads for your business. Or if you prefer, you can use your social media accounts to be a central location for you to do business with both your potential and existing customers.

Identify the most important social media channels for your brand

There are far too many social media websites nowadays. The biggest ones are Facebook, Instagram, Twitter, Snapchat, and Reddit. Depending on the nature of your business and your niche, some social channels may be more preferable than others.

Do your research and find out where you can reach most of your target audience. If the majority of your audience is on Facebook, then be active on Facebook. If most of them are on Pinterest, then make your presence known on Pinterest, and so on.

If you're selling an evergreen product or service that caters to professionals or businesses, then consider having an active presence on LinkedIn.

Identifying the right platforms is important as it's simply not cost-effective to be on channels where you'll see very little return on your investment. So, make sure you do your homework before you create those social media accounts.

Establish your identity across social media and web platforms

As you've learned in the previous chapter, branding is important for your business. Having a social media presence is obviously very important for your branding efforts.

> To establish your social media and web identity, you need to be consistent with your brand colors, your logos, images, and even the tone or language used in your content.

You should project a single and consistent brand for your business so no matter where people find you, they'd recognize your brand anywhere. They shouldn't feel any disconnect as it could turn them off.

For instance, if you're selling a child-friendly product on your website, but on social media you're making controversial posts about kids, then people will be confused about what exactly your brand does.

Presenting a uniform front across your web properties, including social ones, is important to build the perfect identity you want to convey to your audience.

Publish timely and relevant content

Without content, your social media presence will amount to nothing. If you want to gain a sizeable following and you want to be respected by your peers, then you need to publish not just timely, but relevant content as well.

Posting cat memes are great on your personal news feed, but on your brand's social accounts, you have to ask yourself first if cat memes will provide value to your followers.

If you're selling cat-related products, then cat memes could work, but if you're in an entirely different industry, your followers may abandon you. Unless, of course, you find a way to make a cat meme relevant to what your brand is about!

If you have an active blog, don't forget to share it on your social media channels too. That way, your followers know you've published a new post, and they're not missing out on anything valuable.

> *Don't be afraid to ask them to share your content. Asking nicely may give you organic shares for free.*

Don't just post text content – use other media too

Don't hesitate to use visually appealing images to accompany your text posts. Texts are great for conveying information, but as the saying goes, a picture paints a thousand words.

And with ever decreasing attention spans and instant gratification, many people would rather look at an image or watch a video than read lengthy articles.

It's a fact too that images and videos get shared more than text. So, if you want to maximize your organic reach on social media – that is, you're not paying for ads – then use attractive images and videos to grab people's attention.

Don't hesitate to share other people's content

There's no problem sharing other people's content if it adds value to your users. You can even send these third-party sites a direct message or tag them in your post to let them know you've shared their awesome content.

They might even thank you by returning the favor and sharing one of your posts with their followers! It's a win-win situation for the both of you, so don't be afraid to share valuable content even if that content belongs to a direct competitor.

I'm sure if you were in the same situation and a competitor reached out to you to let you know they've shared your content, then chances are you would reciprocate their action, too.

Create a community

Creating a community on social media simply means getting people involved and engaged with your brand. This is why groups and forums work so well. It's because we like to belong to a group of similar-minded people.

When you post something, ask your followers to comment and let their thoughts be known. Ask for their opinion and tell them you'd value their input. Start a discussion on relevant topics, tag people if you need to get the ball rolling.

And don't leave anyone hanging – if anyone asks a question, be there and answer as soon as you can. Don't wait for someone else to chime in. Let people see you're active and engaged with your community.

Being an active part of the community ensures you've truly got a social media presence. You're helping build your business' visibility online by leaving digital footprints on social media.

And if you post valuable content and write smart responses to community discussions, then you'll be seen as an authority figure and thought leader by anyone who follows you on social media.

Pay for ads if you need to

You're not going to get much organic traction when you first start out on social media. In fact, even if you post every day, not too many people will see your updates. If you want to get maximum reach, consider advertising on social media.

Most social media platforms allow you to advertise without breaking the bank. For instance, you can get video views or link clicks on Facebook Ads for mere cents. And with Facebook's superb audience targeting tools, you can reach billions of people in the world!

> *Paying for adverts is one of the quickest ways to establish your social presence and identity.*

If you've got the budget for it, do it just to get a head start. When you begin getting a good number of organic shares on social media, you can stop paying for ads and just focus on growing your traffic organically by providing value to your users.

Are You Ready To Start Building Your Social Media Presence?

Becoming a social media influencer will take a lot of hard work and the road to success isn't always going to be smooth. You'll have rough patches here and there, but if you have a solid plan for establishing your social media presence, then you'd know what pitfalls to avoid.

Being a successful social media influencer is a huge responsibility to your followers. Remember that social media is where people hang out to connect with their family, friends, and acquaintances. It's where people go to unwind after a long day at work.

Don't stress them up by bombarding them with things they didn't sign up for.

Your followers chose to follow you because of your brand and what you bring to the table. They were drawn to you because you offered them something of value.

Continue what you started and give them value often. If you do this, you'll soon find yourself as someone that people look up to, respect and admire. At this point, you'd have firmly established your online identity and social presence.

CHAPTER 7: How To Repurpose Your Content For Various Mediums

Creating content isn't always easy. Sure, you may enjoy writing, recording podcasts or shooting videos, but organizing and researching your content may take you far longer than the actual content creation part. So, how do you go about maximizing your research and letting it last for a long time?

The answer lies with repurposing your content into many different formats. There are a lot of advantages to doing this with not too many downsides. In fact, the only negative aspect of repurposing content is that it will take time or money. Time if you do the repurposing yourself and money if you decide to outsource it.

The Benefits of Repurposing Content

With repurposed content, you need to do less research. And you get a lot more work done in less amount of time. Here are some of the benefits of repurposing content:

Maximize your research

You spend so much time on research that it can get quite frustrating if you know all your hard work is just going into a single piece of content.

Wouldn't it be nice if you can create 5 or maybe even 10 content pieces just from a single hour of research?

For example, if it takes you an hour to research for a piece of content, then it will take you around 5 hours to research for 5 content pieces. However, with content repurposing, you can build off the data you researched in just 1 hour and still come up with 5 content pieces! Essentially, you will be saving about 4 hours of research time.

With this example, I hope you can see just how powerful content repurposing is. Of course, the one-hour research time does not include the actual content creation time.

Depending on the type of content you intend to make, writing or creating the actual content itself may take you far longer than the single hour you spent on researching it.

> *Content repurposing gives your research time more mileage by allowing you to get as much value as possible.*

You no longer need to worry about coming up with new ideas every week – you can instead spend that time thinking of other formats to repurpose your content to.

Visibility in many platforms

If your primary content goes on your blog, then people are only going to be finding out about you by going to your blog. However, if you repurpose your content into other formats and upload these into other platforms, then you're giving your audience a chance to discover you on these other platforms.

For instance, if you repurpose your blog post into a YouTube video, then you'll have access to YouTubers who are interested in your content.

If you convert your blog post into an infographic, then people on Pinterest are going to discover your content which will then allow them to discover your website. If you convert your post into a slide deck, you can upload it to SlideShare to get more eyeballs to your content.

The great thing is these different places are also going to appear on Google so you can have many listings on Google for the same piece of content!

Makes You Look Credible

If people go on Google and see you multiple times, they're going to find you more credible than if they don't see you there at all. Since you're going to be uploading your repurposed content into websites with high domain authority, chances are they're going to get indexed and ranked on Google as well.

The more places people find you at, the bigger your brand appears to be. And since you're repurposing content, then your expertise and your brand's message is going to be in many different places. They'll see you as being an expert, or at least very passionate about your niche.

This helps you become more credible in front of your target audience. And the more credible you appear to be, the more likely it is that people are going to purchase whatever product or service you're selling.

Bring people's attention to less popular content

You'd normally want to repurpose your most popular content pieces to bring it in front of people who may be interested in what you have to say. However, if you also have other content which may not have been as popular with your current audience, then you might want to breathe new life into it by repurposing it and putting it in front of new people. This is especially useful if you're proud of the work you've done on those pieces and you spent a lot of countless nights researching it.

If you feel your current audience didn't appreciate your hard work, then there's no harm in repurposing it to other formats that other people may like.

For instance, if you have a number of blog posts that didn't get as much engagement as you want, you can perhaps try to package it as a free eBook that you can use to drive people to sign up for your mailing list.

Likewise, if you have a well-researched and well-written eBook that didn't get many downloads, then you may want to try repurposing it into a series of blog posts or articles that you can post on your site or social media.

More opportunities for people to link back to your website

Backlinks don't really matter much if you don't care about ranking in search engines. But who wouldn't want to rank organically in Google, right? Just think about it – you're getting free traffic from the world's biggest search engine.

With content repurposing, you can have 1 piece of content converted into a variety of formats. This means that people now have a variety of options to link to your content – they can link to your original article, to your video, to your infographics, to your Facebook post, your Twitter tweet, and so much more.

They're not limited to linking only to your original content. This alone multiplies your backlinking opportunities which could pay off greatly for your website's SEO as Google rewards websites with plenty of high-quality links pointing to them.

How To Repurpose Content Successfully

In order to repurpose your content successfully, you need to carefully plan out your content when you first start writing it. For example, if you're writing a long-form blog post, you might want to break it down into different sections to make the information easily digestible.

You can then repurpose these sections into different formats. It's easier to do it this way as you don't need to do too much editing to get your content to fit another format.

Here are the methods you can follow to repurpose content the right way:

1. Start with an outline

Whether your original content is in blog format or in video format, you need to write down how your content is going to flow. You can just wing it, but that means your content may end up a disorganized mess.

By creating an outline, you get to save time by identifying the points you need to cover in your content. You'd also spend less time editing and reorganizing your work.

Use headings and sub-headings in your outline. And while you're writing down the points you want to cover under each heading, also write down your ideas on how you can reuse that particular section somewhere else.

This system is like hitting two birds with one stone – you plan your original content and how you can repurpose it in one sitting.

2. Have a specific audience in mind for each repurposed content

This point is very important because if you don't plan ahead who you want to see your repurposed content, then you may not be able to serve up the kind of content these people will engage with.

Knowing your audience is very important for any business to succeed. Repurposing content is no different. So, before you repurpose your content, look around and see what kind of content your target audience usually likes in say, YouTube, Pinterest, Reddit, and more.

For instance, if you're targeting middle-aged women in your niche, then you should create videos with this specific audience in mind. Doing this makes you relatable so even if they've never heard of you before or visited your website, your message will resonate with them, and they'll most likely end up following you as well.

If you don't know who your audience is, then you may be hitting blindly in the dark. You could get lucky and find some success, but generally, it's the well thought out content that is made specifically for a certain group of people that succeeds.

3. Use your brand's identity in your repurposed content

The reason you're repurposing content is because you want your brand to be seen in a number of different places. But how can you achieve this if you fail to use your brand's logo, colors, or even font faces?

As we've covered in previous chapters, branding is important for your business' success. Branding helps build your credibility and makes you look trustworthy.

It's important for people to be able to identify your content across many different channels, so do make sure you make it easy for them to do so.

4. Repurpose your content into any of these formats

This isn't a conclusive list by any means, but these formats should give you plenty of head start and allow you expand your reach as quickly as possible. Some may not be a good fit for your niche, so you need to do some research about that as well.

eBooks – if you've got a series of blog posts or articles around the same topic, then you can easily create an eBook. Don't just copy and paste the posts. You still need to go through the eBook with a fine-toothed comb to make sure the content flows well.

You can then use this as a lead magnet or content upgrade for your blog. A high-quality eBook can help position you as an authority in your niche and help you get more leads and sales from both old and new subscribers.

Infographics – the saying a picture paints a thousand words is accurate. An infographic can contain information that may be equivalent to a thousand-word blog post or even 10,000 words.

With infographics, you just need to extract the main points in your content and then transform it into a graphic.

Don't use too many words in your infographic though. Put an emphasis on the graphics part, make it pleasing to the eyes, and upload it to image-oriented sites like Pinterest and Instagram.

Slide Decks – slide decks are quite easy to create on any presentation software like PowerPoint, Keynote or Google Slides. Just like infographics, try not to be too wordy on your slides. Instead, use graphics and icons to emphasize your main points.

This makes your slide decks more easy to understand and will attract more shares than if you just upload a boring text-based slide deck.

Videos – if you've got great content that can be used in a video, then repurpose it as a video. Tutorials and how-to articles are the best types of content to convert to videos. You can even add your video tutorial to your main content – this is not only great for your website's SEO, but you'll get more traffic via your YouTube channel.

Roundup posts – just like with eBooks, if you've got a bunch of posts or articles around the same theme, you should also consider creating a roundup post. This not only allows you to build a longer-form article but it also provides you with a linking opportunity to those old posts.

Internal linking is also great for SEO and encourages your audience to visit other pages on your website.

Podcasts – podcasts are great for people who are always on the go and value their productivity and efficiency. With a podcast, you can just read out your content and record with a good quality microphone. With a bit of editing, you're done, and you can then upload it to your preferred podcasting platform.

Again, there are many other content types you can repurpose your content to. Check out what your competitors are doing, or you can ask your audience for their input. It wouldn't hurt to ask them a few questions, and you just might receive some golden nuggets in return!

CHAPTER 6: How To Create Valuable Content That Truly Sticks

In the online world, you will often read or hear these words, "content is king." This is why many businesses have started to employ content marketing strategies by putting up blogs on their sites and posting their content in many different places.

Publishing valuable content that actually helps people is not only good for your brand's SEO, but it also encourages engagement with your audience. It also sets you up as an authority or thought leader in your niche, which in turn leads to new sales for your business.

The Most Popular Types Of Content You Can Use

Content can come in many forms. It can be in text format like in articles or blog posts, it can be in video format like those you see in YouTube videos, or it can be in an audio format like those you listen to on podcasts.

With so much competition nowadays, people are always coming up with new ways to make their content stand out. In this section I'll show you the most popular types of content you can use to promote your evergreen product:

Articles or blog posts

These text-based content are evergreen forms of content that some people will always favor. Search engines, for one, use your written content to rank various pages of your website.

Research has also shown that businesses who actively blog get more traffic to their sites than those who don't.

Informative articles, how-to posts, product reviews, and more, are what usually brings people over to your website. People read your content, and they make decisions based on the information you present to them.

Videos

There are many video platforms available, but I'm sure the first thing that popped into your mind was YouTube. YouTube is the second biggest search engine, right after Google. People go on YouTube to watch all sorts of things.

For your evergreen business, YouTube video marketing has a lot of benefits for you. You can make videos telling people how to use your product in the real world, or you can show them why your product is better than your competitors.

This is the sort of valuable content that may prove popular with your followers.

Podcasts

Podcasts have become quite popular in recent years. Many people love podcasts because it allows them to consume content even when they're driving or working out at the gym. In short, it allows people to multi-task.

If you make podcasts as part of your content marketing strategy, you will appreciate the fact that creating it is as easy as recording yourself speaking on a microphone.

You can quickly establish yourself as a thought leader in your industry if you provide a lot of value to your listeners.

Infographics

Infographics can cost you a pretty penny if you don't know how to make it yourself. But people love infographics as it's far easier to consume than reading two pages of text that contain the same information!

In addition to providing valuable content at one glance, people can also easily link to your infographic when they mention it in their posts. This gives you plenty of backlinking opportunities which is great for your website's SEO.

Infographics are also quite popular on social media, so don't forget to share it on your social media channels and ask your followers to share it with their network as well!

The 5 Ingredients That Make Content Great

Before I teach you how to create content that truly sticks, let me show you first these five 'ingredients' that define what great content is.

It's original

Google hates duplicate content. And so do your readers. If you want people to continue following you, it's best to stand out from the crowd. Don't just copy and paste other people's content because it can get you in a lot of trouble.

Also, don't even think of using robots or content spinners to create spun content. This just results to more garbage content on the Internet.

If you truly want your content to be great, then you need to create original content. And by original, I don't mean rehashed. If you want to establish yourself as an authority in your niche, then you need to take the time to write something that not many other people know.

Or if you don't have the expertise, then you can outsource it to someone who actually knows the subject.

> *The point is that people, and search engines, will reward you in the long run for taking the time to make original content.*

It's actionable

I'm sure you've come across articles that were well-written but kept you hanging at the end. Why? Because there's no call to action or the content itself wasn't actionable at all. What you just read doesn't tell you what you're supposed to do so it leaves you confused.

If you want people to recognize your content as being great, then you're going to have to give out actionable advice or tips in your content.

You don't have to give them a step-by-step breakdown, but your content should at least make it easy to identify what your audience needs to do to apply the information you're giving them.

It's got a great headline

The headline is the first thing people see when they come upon your content. They're not going to jump into the body, no. They're going to read what your headline is all about and only then will they decide if they want to continue reading.

In essence, a great headline is what makes your reader want to continue. If you wrote a generic and boring headline, your readers might not want to go far enough to read the first paragraph. They'd just close the browser tab and move on to the next website.

It solves a pain point

People will check out your content if they think you can help them. If you're offering the solution to a problem or you have the answer to their questions, then they're going to check out your content. But nowadays, people don't just want answers.

They want answers fast. They want answers immediately.

Even if you do have the answers to their questions, if they can't find it quickly, they're going to leave and look somewhere else. Make sure you structure your content in such a way that your audience can immediately see what they came to find.

It's written in a language your audience understands

This is an important ingredient for making great content. First of all, you need to know who your audience is so you know the kind of language they use, their slangs and terminology.

If your content is geared primarily towards millennials, then use their language. Don't use difficult words that are more fit for people in the academe.

By using their language, you're making your content relatable. You're making it easy for people to trust you and they'd easily welcome you into their community because you belong. Your language will tell them that you're one of them.

How To Create Content That Sticks

Now that you know the different kinds of content you can use as well as the ingredients that make a piece of content great, it's time to show you how you can create content that will truly stick or resonate with your audience.

1. Understand your audience's journey

When creating content, it's important to identify or recognize the stage your target audience will be at in your sales funnel. For example, if you want to bring your brand in front of a new or cold audience, you're not going to sell to them immediately.

You need to warm them up first so they'll trust you. You need to position yourself as an authority or as an expert so they'll move further down your funnel. On the customer side of things, it's called their journey.

But on the marketing side, it's more commonly known as the sales funnel. As your customer continues with their journey, they're moving further down your funnel.

Traditionally, there are 5 stages in a funnel:

Awareness
Engagement
Discovery
Purchase
Retention

You don't want to serve up the same kind of content to people who are just in the awareness stage. Likewise, for those in the purchase stage, you don't want to bring them back to the awareness or engagement stage as these people are now ready to buy from you.

2. Make your content relevant

If you know where your customers are on their journey, then it's easy for you to create relevant content.

> *If they don't know you yet, then try to position yourself as someone they can trust by publishing content that cements your authority in your niche.*

But don't let your content by about you. Let it be about your customers or your audience. If you talk too much about yourself, it will turn people off your brand. No one wants to listen to people who talk too much about themselves.

It's just like going on a first date with a stranger, you wouldn't want to go out with them again if they talked too much about themselves, right? The same goes for your content.

Make your audience feel special by addressing their concerns and their questions. Ask yourself if your content answers the question, "What's in it for my customers?"

It's important to give the right answer because when you capture their attention and their emotions, then you've successfully created content that really sticks with your audience.

3. Know who your audience is

Knowing who your target audience is important so you can create relevant content for them. If you have no idea who your main demographic is then you'd be publishing content that may be a hit or miss with your audience.

You spend a lot of time creating content, so you want to make the most of it. This is why knowing who your target audience is is so important to your success.

In fact, some marketers recommend creating customer avatars and placing them somewhere you can see them all the time. When you're creating your content, you can look at your avatar and try to put yourself in their shoes.

If you're writing for moms, then you have to think like a mom. Ask yourself if the moms who are going to read your content will find it useful. Will they be able to relate? If you do this, you not only make your content relevant, but you also create content that will resonate with them.

Knowing who your audience is will also help you use the kind of language your audience uses just like I've mentioned in the previous section. For moms, you'd have to use words that would appeal to moms.

Placing a call to action in the middle or end of your valuable content is important. If you are targeting people in the awareness stage, then put a call to action that will help move them down the next stage in your funnel.

If you think they're ready to move to the buying stage, then create appropriate content for this set of audience.

> When choosing which call to action to use, you need to put yourself again in your audience's shoes.

With a bit of psychology, you can connect with your audience.

For example, for those who have just stumbled upon your content for the first time, you should encourage them to sign up to your mailing list. If you don't have a mailing list, you need to start one as soon as possible.

By joining your list, you have another avenue to get in touch with them and bring them back to your website again and again. If you continue to give people value, they'd be willing to part with their hard-earned cash and buy whatever product or service you're recommending.

Are You Ready To Start Creating Awesome Content?

Use all the tips I've shared in this chapter to create your content. If you're new to content creation, just think of it as telling stories to your audience –

make it engaging and make it actionable. To not lose your audience's interest, perhaps try using a bit of humor if it fits your niche.

To make sure you publish content regularly, create a content schedule and do your best to stick to that schedule. It will be hard at first, but with a bit of practice, creating valuable content that resonates with your audience will soon become easy for you.

CHAPTER 8: How To Generate Traffic From Multiple Sources

When you're a content creator, seeing people consume your content can bring you a lot of joy. These people – your audience – are on their way to bringing you profits, so you need to take care of them while they're on your site.

They're there for a reason – you promised to help them with something they need help with. But how do you get people to visit your site in the first place? This is what you're going to learn in this chapter.

Google Traffic Is Great (But It's Not The Only One)

When people first set up their websites, they automatically assume people are going to find them on Google right away. But search engines are complicated, and with the sheer number of live websites on the world wide web, you have plenty of competition.

Not everyone can be on the first page of Google. In fact, only ten websites appear on every page of search results (this is organic, paid listings are not included). If you want to check out other sites, you'd have to scroll all the way down and click on Next to go to the next page.

Ranking on the first page of Google can bring you plenty of free organic traffic. It's free because you're not paying Google anything to appear on the first page.

Organic because people are finding you of their own accord on Google. But getting to this stage is difficult – and even if you do your SEO right, you may still not end up on the first page of Google.

In short, ranking on Google is hard work, and if you depend on Google traffic, you could be waiting for nothing and your business will die if you don't get traffic to sustain it.

So, if you can't depend on Google, how are you going to get people over to your website? Well, there are two ways to go about generating traffic – by paying for it and by posting valuable content on free platforms.

Paid Traffic Versus Free Traffic

Luckily for you and me, Google is not the only game in town. Paid traffic will, of course, cost you some money, but it doesn't have to cost you an arm and a leg. On the other hand, generating free traffic is not as hard as it once was thanks mainly to social media but you'd still need to do plenty of work.

With free traffic, you may not get a constant stream of people instantly, and it may take some time to get to that point. But at least you're being proactive in seeking out people who may be interested in your content.

That's way better than doing nothing and waiting for your site to rank on Google!

Pros and Cons of Paid Traffic

If you've got the money to burn, then you may want to consider paying for traffic. Not only do you get traffic instantly, but you can also buy quality traffic for cents on the dollar.

Take, for instance, Facebook Ads. Facebook marketers swear by the effectiveness of Facebook Ads and its incomparable audience targeting options. Many marketers are profiting handsomely with Facebook Ads.

With over 2 billion active users on the platform, you'll most probably run out of money first before you run out of people to target!

With paid traffic, there are generally 3 options to choose from:

Cost per click (CPC) – you only pay every time someone clicks on your ad

Cost per mille (CPM) – you pay per 1,000 views regardless of whether people clicked on your ad or not

Fixed rate – you pay this amount regardless of the number of people who clicked or viewed your ad

The thing with paid ads is that you can set up your website or landing page today, pay for ads, and get traffic instantly. You don't need to wait for days, weeks or months for people to visit your site.

Just get an eye-catching advert in front of your target audience, and you can assess if you've got a winner or a loser on your hands!

With instant traffic comes the possibility of instant profits. If you've got a great offer for your audience, and you're going to be profiting $100 per sale, wouldn't you be willing to pay $1 or even $10 per click?

Most paid traffic enthusiasts will tell you to do the math, and if your math tells you that you're in the green, then there's no point wasting time waiting for your site to rank on Google. Just dive right in and invest in paid traffic!

The downside with paid traffic, of course, is that you could lose your money on ads that won't show any ROI (return on investment) for you.

You'd have to constantly monitor your traffic and test your ads until you find the best-performing ones. This can get stressful. And once you stop paying for traffic, then that traffic stops coming to your site.

Think paid traffic is too risky for you? Read the next section for tips on how to generate traffic from multiple, free sources.

Pros and Cons of Free Traffic

Not everyone will have the money or the stomach to risk their hard-earned money on ads that may or may not return any profits for them. If you belong to this group, then generating free traffic is your best bet for getting people to head over to your website.

There are many ways to generate free traffic. Most free methods will take some time before people show up on your website. However, the good thing is that your post or comment will stay on that free site for as long as the site lives.

Essentially, you'll be doing the hard work once and reap the profits for a long time to come. This is obviously great as it could bring you free traffic for many years. And if your free traffic converts well then this could contribute significantly to your passive income.

The caveat with free traffic, however, is that you're paying with your time. If you value your time, then you may wish to consider paid traffic instead. Additionally, success is also not guaranteed so your hard work may go to waste eventually.

If you don't have a content strategy in place, then your free traffic generation strategy would be equivalent to building your business on a house of cards.

To help ensure your free traffic generation strategies will actually pay off after some time, then read the next section for ideas on where to source free quality traffic for your website.

How To Generate Free Traffic From Multiple Sources

In the previous chapter, we discussed how to repurpose content, and I showed you the best content types you can reformat your main content to. I'm mentioning this here because you're going to be using those repurposed contents to generate free traffic from many different platforms!

1. Be active on social media

There are plenty of reasons why companies – big and small – target social media users. This is because people spend a lot of their time on these sites.

Facebook alone has 2 billion active users every month and thousands more create accounts every single day. Next to SEO, social media marketing is the next best way to drive free traffic to your website.

2. Answer questions on sites like Quora and Yahoo Answers

Sites like these have high domain authority. This is why you'll notice that there are many posts which appear on the first page Google search results, especially for long tail keywords.

If you want to get a share of the traffic, be helpful and provide thoughtful answers to questions about your niche. Don't leave one-liners. If you want people to upvote your answers, then you need to write detailed and thorough answers as much as possible.

3. Engage heavily in popular forums in your niche

Some people like to spam forums with links to their website. People hate spammers like that! So, if you don't want to get kicked out, make sure you add value to discussions in your forum. Make yourself well-known in the community.

Once you've established yourself as someone who knows what they're talking about, then slowly ease into promoting yourself or your website. Don't be too salesy though – like I said people hate that kind of behavior.

4. YouTube marketing

YouTube is the second biggest search engine right after Google. And YouTube videos often rank high in Google search results especially for tutorials and how-to queries. If you want your videos to rank, and bring you free traffic to your website, you need to follow a few basic video SEOs.

Also, don't spam YouTube with copied and pasted content. Try to be as helpful as possible and offer original content that will help you win over your viewers.

5. Engage with your podcast listeners

To succeed in podcasting, you need to provide valuable content to your listeners. Having a great voice is a plus, but ultimately it's going to be your content that really matters. You can also try and reach out to other podcasters and interview them on your podcast to try and extend your reach.

Lastly, don't just say adios at the end of your podcast – make sure you include a call to action as well!

6. Guest post on authority sites in your niche

Guest posting is a great way to introduce yourself to other people's audiences. If you write a super valuable post and that site's followers love your content, then chances are they're going to want to follow you as well.

This not only brings you an additional stream of free traffic, you also normally get a free backlink back to your website. If your guest post lives on a high domain authority site, then that backlink can do wonders for your website's SEO!

7. Email your list

If you've already got an email list, don't forget about them. If you're taking a lot of time promoting your brand on other people's websites to get in front of new audiences, then you should all the more prioritize the people who already trust you.

Don't spam them with offers though. Instead, continue giving them valuable content, so they don't hit that unsubscribe or worse, that spam button.

8. Upload your slide decks to SlideShare and similar sites

If you've repurposed your content into slide decks, then you can upload it to sites like SlideShare. You'll get traffic from people who search for content like yours on those sites, plus you'll even get a free backlink. Again, this is great for your website's SEO.

9. Upload your images to photo sharing sites like Instagram

Who doesn't love photos especially high-quality ones? If you want to endear yourself to your followers, then regularly upload photos relevant to your brand or business.

Depending on your niche and the nature of your evergreen product, it is very much possible to drive traffic from Instagram to your website. You just need to make your images appealing and highly relevant to your target audience.

10. Leave thoughtful comments on other people's blogs

Some people say blog commenting is dead. If you spam blogs, then yes, it's true. But if you leave thoughtful comments that actually add value to the original post, then people are going to be curious about you.

Additionally, it may get you in good graces with the blog owner, and you can start building a relationship with them.

11. Promote discount codes or coupons on different sites

People love freebies and discounts. If they think they're getting a good deal over a product they really want, then they're going to bite whatever it is you're offering. You can promote your offers and codes on your own website, or you can post it on your social media channels.

If you do it right, you can soon expect people to visit your website to take advantage of your offer!

Want Even More Free Traffic? Offer Plenty Of Value Wherever Possible!

There are plenty of different ways to generate free traffic. The common method to get good quality free traffic is by offering people plenty of value. There are plenty of platforms to choose from, and you don't always have to do what everyone is doing.

In fact, you can think outside the box to come up with creative ways to encourage people to visit your website. When you find a free traffic source that not many people know about, then you'll feel like you've won the jackpot!

CHAPTER 9: How To Start Building Your Email List

One of the best ways to grow your evergreen business is by building your email list. An email list is simply a list of people's email addresses – people who've chosen to subscribe to your list because you offered something of value to them.

In this chapter, you're going to be learning why you need an email list. I'll also give you plenty of ideas on how you can build your list using both free and paid methods.

Why You Need An Email List

You'll often hear marketers say that the money is in the list. With just a few minutes work, they can contact their email list and get thousands of dollars of sales in just a few hours! Wouldn't you want to do the same? I bet you would!

Here are more reasons why you need an email list if you want your business to grow.

It's your very own online asset

In the online world, you're going to be at the mercy of many web giants who can take your business away from you in an instant. Here's a case in point:

You spend months working on moving your website's rank up Google's search results. You write thousands of words of valuable content to guest post in an authoritative site with excellent domain authority. You follow white-hat SEO techniques and don't mess around with blackhat SEO.

When your site finally reaches the top spot for your target keyword, a competitor decides to employ some shady tactics so they can steal your spot. And in a matter of hours, Google penalizes you for something you didn't do.

> *You could lose everything you worked hard for because you're literally at the mercy of Google.*

With a drastic decline in organic search traffic, you decide to try social media marketing. You pay for adverts on Facebook or Instagram just to get people to visit your website because you know Facebook's organic reach is very unpredictable.

It works very well and you start seeing some sales again, and you get your hopes up that this time it's going to be okay. Until the very same invisible competitor figured out what you were doing and decided to smear your reputation on social media.

I know my example is a bit extreme but can you see where this is going? You don't have control over your Google rankings. Nor do you have control over your social media assets.

What you do control, however, is your website and your email list, provided you own your domain name and pay for your own hosting (you don't own your website if you host it on a free hosting service).

With your two web properties – website and email list – you're free to do as you please with them.

It's easier to sell to people who already know you

Selling to a cold audience is hard. Try pitching to random strangers on a busy street, and you'd probably get reported to the police for harassment.

To increase your chances of making a sale, you'd need to warm up your customers first to get them to trust you. Offer them something of value – a free trial perhaps – and if they like your product, they'd be more likely to buy it.

The same idea goes for email lists. When people sign up to your list, it's because they like you or they trust you on some level. So when you sell them something via email, they'll be more likely to respond positively to your call to action.

Generating profits from your mailing list is important for your business. But don't make every email a sales pitch for your own products or any other product you're affiliated with. Use your list to build a relationship with your audience. Build on the trust they've already placed in you by continuing to offer them value.

Don't make your subscribers regret signing up to your list. If you give them value, they'll be more likely to remain on your list. If you spam them with nothing but sales offers, they'd probably hit the Spam or Block button, and your emails will never see their inbox ever again.

Remember to offer value to your subscribers, and you'll be rewarded with profits you can only imagine right now!

You can easily drive traffic back to your website

In my example earlier, I showed you why you can't rely on Google and social media to give you free traffic. But if you have your very own mailing list, and a sizeable one I might add, then you can simply tell your subscribers to go check out your new post every time you publish one!

Awesome, right?

Of course, what you publish must be relevant to what your subscribers initially signed up for. If you cover a lot of different niches on your site, then it's important that you consider segregating your list.

For example, if you create evergreen products in the health, love and wealth niches then you have to create 3 different email lists. One list for people interested in the health niche, another for people interested in your love niche products, and a third one for those who are interested in becoming wealthy.

Segregating your list will mean you'd have to work thrice as hard to grow your list, but sooner or later, you'll amass a good number of subscribers per list. And your subscribers will be more than happy to read your emails because it's relevant to them.

If you group your lists this way, then you need to make sure you only send relevant content to the right list. Otherwise, you run the risk of upsetting some subscribers which could result to people unsubscribing from your list.

However, if you only send them niche-related emails and it's something that interests them, then they'd be more likely to follow your email's call to action and go check out your new post on your website.

Steps To Build Your Email List The Right Way

In this section, I'm going to cover the steps you can follow to create a high-quality email list. Note that I'm mentioning quality here because if you end up with a low-quality list, then it's probably not going to be worth the time and effort building that list in the first place.

1. Offer something so valuable that your audience will feel compelled to sign up

You probably visited hundreds of websites in the last week or so. And I daresay a good number of those sites had an email opt-in form somewhere.

Probably a pop-up or in the sidebar, asking you to enter your email address so you can receive a free eBook or something. Can you remember how many websites you chose to sign up for? And do you remember why you chose to do so?

For most people, we normally only sign up for email lists which offer a tempting 'bribe.' We don't want to receive 'free updates.' You can't just put up an opt-in form anywhere and ask people to enter their email address. That strategy probably worked 5 years ago but not today.

Today, if you want people to join your list, you'd have to offer them something truly valuable. Something that will make them go, *"Oh wow, this is really useful to me. I'd love to get my hands on that! Okay, here I go. I'm typing in my real email address now. I can't wait to read this stuff!"*

To get email subscribers, you need to think carefully about how you're going to lure them in to sign up for your list. Should you offer a free eBook, a free video course, a free Skype consult? Whatever you decide on, put yourself in their shoes. Would YOU sign up for your list?

If you answered yes, then you're off to a good start. But if you answered no, then you need to go back to the drawing board and review your content strategy again. No one ever said building a list is easy.

You'd have to work hard to get people's email addresses. By giving them something really useful or helpful, you're increasing your chances of getting them to sign up.

The caveat, of course, is that not everyone would want to sign up for your list no matter how great your free eBook or video course is. That's normal. But with a high-quality offer on the table, your opt-in rates will be so much higher than if you didn't carefully think things through.

2. Put your opt-in forms in high-converting places on your website

Ad banner blindness is a real thing. And so is email opt-in form blindness. If you're using a standard opt-in form with a generic design, no one's going to pay any attention to it.

It may just as well be invisible with the dismal opt-in rates you're going to get. It's also just a waste of valuable website real estate.

Website design can vary widely from one site to another. But generally, these are the top places most website owners report as giving them higher-than-average opt-in rates:

Top of the sidebar – your sidebar can be on the left or right side of the page. Wherever it is, try adding an opt-in form at the top of the sidebar. Heatmaps show sidebars get good activity so don't be afraid to try this option.

Splash page – this is the first thing your site visitors will see on your website. Make it clear to them what the benefits are if they sign up for your list. You can use a 'start here' sign, a smiling photo of yourself or your free giveaway, or a testimonial from a happy subscriber or customer.

Header – your website's header is the one place everyone sees no matter where they are on your website. It's above the fold, so people don't need to scroll down to see your opt-in form. With a combination of a great offer and opt-in form design, you may get more people to opt-in to your list!

Within your blog posts – if you don't have a blog on your website, you're losing out. Publishing high-quality content regularly on your blog will help establish your authority and attract more people to follow your brand.

Add your opt-in form preferably in the middle or bottom of your posts. This way, people would already have read your content, so you know when they sign up, they're interested in what you have to offer.

Timed pop-up or lightbox – you can set your opt-in form to appear after a certain amount of time – say 1 or 2 minutes. This allows your visitors to look around your site for a bit and get to know you better before you ask them to sign up.

Most people normally just close pop-ups that appear as soon as they land on a website, but timed pop-ups allow people to get acquainted with your brand first.

The opt-in rates for any of these locations will vary from niche to niche. You'd have to do a lot of tests to find the spot that will work best for your website.

3. Drive highly targeted traffic to your website's opt-in form

The last step you need to do to get people to sign up to your list is to drive traffic to your website. Without traffic, you don't get to build an email list. But don't just invite anyone to sign up to your list.

Remember, you want to build a high-quality list full of people who are very interested in you, your products, or your services.

A strategy most successful marketers employ is they first create a buyer persona or a profile of a person most likely to benefit from their business.

So, if you're targeting middle-aged women with 1 to 2 kids, then you have to reach out to this audience. You can use paid and free traffic generation methods to do this.

In the previous chapter, I showed you different methods to generate traffic using paid and free traffic sources. Use whatever method you're most comfortable with.

The important thing is that you know exactly who to target, so you don't waste too much time and money. Having a good-sized mailing list composed of your ideal audience will bring you plenty of profits in the long run.

Don't forget to offer your subscribers plenty of value and don't think of them as your human cash cards whenever you need to make some money. Treat your subscribers as your friends, and you'll be justly rewarded with everlasting profits!

CHAPTER 10: How To Create And Sell Your Very Own Evergreen Course

If you're passionate about something and you want to share it with the world, then you might want to consider creating your very own evergreen course.

You may think no one's going to pay you for sharing information, but you'd be surprised to know how many first-time entrepreneurs (who've never sold a single thing online) successfully sold their first course!

If you want to experience launching a successful online course, then read on because, in this chapter, you're going to learn exactly how you can create your very own course and generate passive income for years to come!

Why You Should Create and Sell Your Very Own Course

Here are a few reasons why you should consider creating and selling your very own online course if you want to generate everlasting, passive profits.

1. There is a huge demand for online courses

The online course market is worth billions of dollars annually. And it doesn't look like it's going to slow down anytime soon. People love the fact that they can learn new things in the comfort of their homes, and study at their own pace.

They don't need to go to school on weekdays or weekends, just to listen to someone drone on and on about theory. The truth is, in most schools, you don't get to choose who your teacher is going to be. So, it's usually plain luck if you get an amazing teacher to handle your class.

Anyway, the point is that with most online courses, people already have an idea who the teacher is going to be. They know exactly what they're going to learn.

And people can choose to buy a course that only discusses the things they need to know – no fluff and unnecessary introductions and background chatter. They can choose to enroll in a beginner course, an intermediate course, or an advanced course.

And that's where you come in. Depending on your level of expertise and the audience demographic you want to reach, you can choose to create a course that's geared for beginners or more advanced students.

2. It can provide you with passive income

Want to make money while you sleep? Or while you're away on vacation in the Caribbean? Or anywhere remote, for that matter? When you sell your own online course, this is very much possible.

> *In fact, many entrepreneurs have successfully created passive income streams for themselves just by selling online courses.*

You can create your course in January, start selling it in February, and from that point forward you could be earning money day in and day out. You don't even need to edit your course again.

Though, of course, if you want your course to continue selling, then you should definitely want to spend a lot of time promoting it!

3. You can create a course on practically anything you want!

Do yourself a favor and check out platforms that sell online courses. You'll notice that topics can range from the most basic to the most advanced tutorials on many different subjects.

What this means for you is if you've got something to teach, then you can create a course for that!

If you love to cook, you can create a course on how to bake desserts using a special technique. If you love taking photos, you can create a course on photography. If you love designing clothes, and you want to share your advanced techniques, then you can sell your own course on this subject as well.

You can design your course to cater only to beginners or advanced students. Or if you want, you can create a comprehensive course that will take people from being absolute newbies to experts! The choice is totally up to you.

> *Don't underestimate people's ability and willingness to pay for your knowledge.*

If you market your course as something that can help your students fix a problem, or improve their skills, or address a very specific pain point, then you'd have a very profitable course on your hands.

How To Get Started With Creating And Selling Your Own Evergreen Course

Before you start creating your online course, it's important to put yourself in your students' shoes. Would they find your course valuable? Would they learn something new and actionable from you?

Do you care about their learning experience or are you only out to line your pockets with their money?

Always remember that if you want Endless Internet Profits, you need to provide as much value as possible to your audience. If you fail to do this, and only think about yourself, then your business is not going to last.

Helping people should be your top priority whether you create a video course, a text-based course, an audio course, etc.

Here's a step by step guide to help you start creating your first course:

1. Choose a profitable evergreen topic

While you can choose to create a course on any subject you want, you want to make sure you'll actually have enough people interested in your topic.

Helping people is important, but since you're building a business, you should also want to see a return on your investment and generate a healthy profit.

There are quite a few ways to find a profitable topic:

Check if there are existing courses on the topic you want to cover. If there are, and it's selling, then that's a good sign. It simply means there's a demand for that topic, and you can create a much better course than your competitors.

Do keyword research to find out how many people are searching for your topic. If you've got a decent number of monthly searches, and there aren't enough resources on the subject, then you might be on to something!

Seek out forums in the niche you want to cover and see what kind of problems people are having with. Forums are literally a gold mine so be sure to go through all the threads containing your topic. Create a list of target problems and then create a course around that.

Lastly, I mentioned 'evergreen' because you want to create a passive income stream, right? If you choose a non-evergreen niche like technology, then your course will become obsolete as soon as that technology becomes outdated.

But with evergreen niches, you don't need to worry about all that. Your course could still be selling decades after you launched it!

2. Test and check if your topic is indeed profitable

This step is very important if you want to avoid wasting your time and money on building a course no one will buy. You can ask the opinion of your family and friends, but they'd probably be biased and tell you what you want to hear – that your course is great and it's going to sell like hotcakes.

But if you want to get real world feedback from people you're interested in selling your course to, then you can try creating a survey and have your target audience answer it.

How?

If you've got an email list, you can simply ask them to answer your quick survey. If you don't have a list, then you need to get creative.

You can maybe create a mini-course on the subject you want to sell and use it as an email opt-in. Then drive traffic to your mini-course.

Track how many people visited your site and compare it to the number of people who actually signed up.

If you get a nice conversion rate, then it means your course can be profitable. If you get very low sign up rates, then maybe your idea isn't very sellable. Or you simply didn't target the right people. Or maybe you need to write better copy to encourage prospects to sign up.

Try split testing so you can make an informed decision on whether to continue with your course or just totally forget about it.

3. Create a course outline and write your content

At this point, you should already know your course has an audience waiting to be sold to. The next step you need to do is plan out how you're going to structure your course.

Creating a detailed outline is very important as you can clearly see which areas you need to cover. Cover the main points in your course – no need to go crazy on the details yet.

The important thing is you need to get your audience's problem solved, and you need to make sure your course answers that problem thoroughly.

Break your course into small "bite-sized" sections. Group similar concepts together. Don't allow your ideas to be all over the place. Your audience will appreciate you taking the time to make things easy enough for them to understand.

Once you've finished the outline, take a moment to review it. Ask yourself if you left anything out, and if you think it's got all the details to help your intended audience. Only then should you start working on the content.

Don't get too hung up on getting the perfect eBook cover, or the perfect lighting for your videos, or how you're going to sound in your audio recording.

Some successful entrepreneurs' first-ever courses were shot on their smartphone or their laptop's webcam! Whatever content type you choose to go with, your students are going to pay you for your content and your knowledge.

4. Upload your course to your website or a third-party learning platform

Now that you've successfully created a great course, it's time to upload it online so you can start selling it.

There are generally 3 types of places where you can sell your course:

Your own website – having your own course on your own web property gives you the most control over your product. You can choose your own design and set your own price. You don't have to give anyone a share of your profits, you get to keep everything!

If you use WordPress, you can simply use a plugin to manage your course and your payments, and you can be in business in a matter of hours!

Third-party hosted platforms – if you don't have your own website, or you don't want to be bothered with setting it up on your own, you can simply host your course on a third-party platform.

These platforms make it easy for you to upload and manage your course, but they do come at a price. Some require a monthly or annual subscription while some require a certain percentage of your sales.

Online learning marketplaces – sites like these have become popular in recent years. If you want to get your course in front of millions of people, then this is the best place for your course. However, the downside is that you have very little control over your course once you upload it.

Most platforms also place a limit on course prices, and they even take a cut of your earnings so be sure to keep this information in mind.

5. Promote your course to your target audience

Since you've already identified your audience before you even started creating your course, it's now time to let them know about your course and how it can help solve their pain point!

If you've got an email list like I discussed in Step 2, then you have to email them now. Let them know how they can benefit from your course and guide them to where they can buy it.

> *Make them feel special, offer them something nice as an existing subscriber – maybe a discount code or a free preview.*

You can also use free and paid methods to drive traffic to your course. There are many ways you can generate traffic but make sure you target the right audience, so you get good conversion rates.

Use proven marketing strategies to encourage your target audience to buy your course. Know how a sales funnel works so you can entice your leads or prospects to become paying customers.

And remember to ask them to opt-in to your email list so you can contact them again later on.

Are You Ready To Start Selling Your Evergreen Course?

An evergreen course is one of the best ways to generate passive income. While you do need to put in a LOT of work to make your course awesome, you just need to remember the fact that you only need to do the hard work once.

You can create a course in less than a week and have it generate sales for many years. Imagine if you are selling several evergreen courses – you can live the life you've always dreamed of and spend your time doing what you love the most!